This family photo book belongs to

. . . .

Also by Anchal Verma

My Weekly French Journal: A Year-52-week Goal Tracking Journal for French learners with French proverbs, French tongue twisters, a list of useful French expressions and plenty of other bonus material

My French Notebook: Ruled 6 sections Notebook/Diary with some useful French expressions

My Language Notebook : Ruled 6 sections Notebook with some useful expressions in different languages

French Vocabulary Bank: English-French bilingual vocabulary book of essential French words and phrases

Littérature Fantastique Belge et Belgitude : Étude des nouvelles fantastiques de Jean Ray

For more information about Anchal Verma and her books, visit her website at https://anchalverma.com/

My family

Ma
famille (Mah
fam-ee)

STICK PHOTO HERE

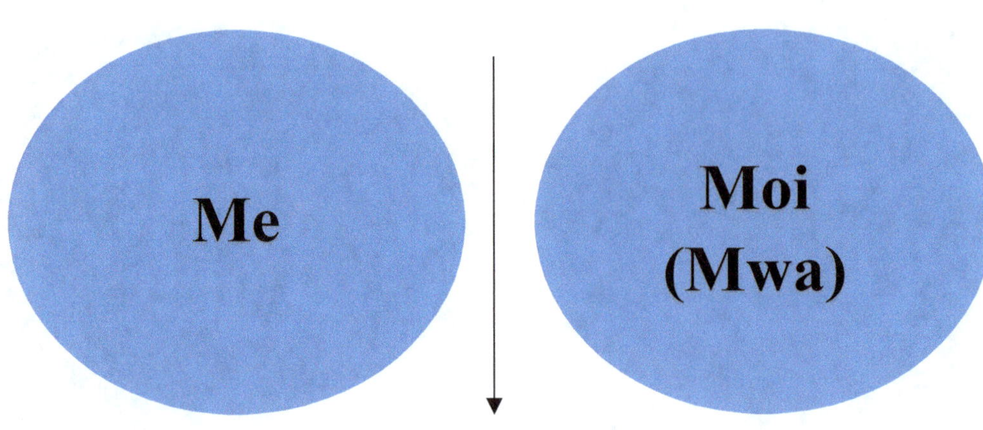

STICK PHOTO HERE

My name is

....

Je m'appelle
(Zhuh mah-pel)

....

My mother
Ma mère (Mah mair)
STICK PHOTO HERE

Her name is

....

Elle s'appelle
(Ell sah-pel)

....

STICK PHOTO HERE

His name is

. . . .

Il s'appelle
(Eel sah-pel)

. . . .

My
brother

Mon frère
(Mohn
frair)

STICK PHOTO HERE

His name is

....

Il s'appelle
(Eel sah-pel)

....

STICK PHOTO HERE

Her name is

....

Elle s'appelle
(Ell sah-pel)

....

My
grandmother

Ma
grand-mère
(Mah groh-mair)

STICK PHOTO HERE

Her name is

....

Elle s'appelle
(Ell sah-pel)

....

My grandmother

Ma grand-mère (Mah groh-mair)

STICK PHOTO HERE

Her name is

....

Elle s'appelle
(Ell sah-pel)

....

My grandfather

**Mon
grand-père
(Mohn groh-pair)**

STICK PHOTO HERE

His name is

....

Il s'appelle
(Eel sah-pel)

....

My grandfather

**Mon
grand-père
(Mohn groh-pair)**

STICK PHOTO HERE

His name is

. . . .

Il s'appelle
(Eel sah-pel)

. . . .

<table>
<tr><td>

My uncle

</td><td>

Mon oncle (Mohn ohnkl)

</td></tr>
</table>

STICK PHOTO HERE

His name is

. . . .

Il s'appelle
(Eel sah-pel)

. . . .

My uncle

Mon oncle (Mohn ohnkl)

STICK PHOTO HERE

His name is

....

Il s'appelle
(Eel sah-pel)

....

My aunt

Ma tante (Mah tont)

STICK PHOTO HERE

Her name is

....

Elle s'appelle
(Ell sah-pel)

....

My aunt

Ma tante (Mah tont)

STICK PHOTO HERE

Her name is

....

Elle s'appelle
(Ell sah-pel)

....

My cousin (brother)

Mon cousin (Mohn koo-zah)

STICK PHOTO HERE

His name is

. . . .

Il s'appelle
(Eel sah-pel)

. . . .

My cousin (sister)

Ma cousine (Mah koo-zeen)

STICK PHOTO HERE

Her name is

....

Elle s'appelle
(Ell sah-pel)

....

www.ingramcontent.com/pod-product-compliance
Lightning Source LLC
LaVergne TN
LVHW080505200726
843509LV00008B/377